CONTENTS

THE MAGIC MOMENT

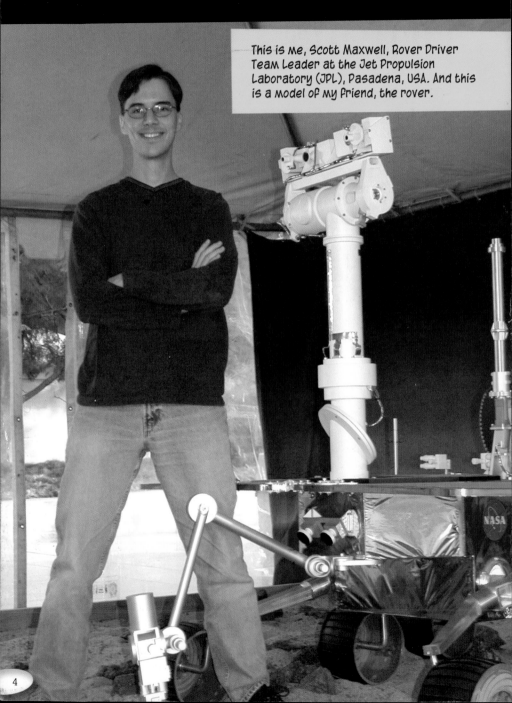

This is me, Scott Maxwell, Rover Driver Team Leader at the Jet Propulsion Laboratory (JPL), Pasadena, USA. And this is a model of my friend, the rover.

THE COOLEST JOBS ON THE PLANET

MARS ROVER DRIVER

Scott Maxwell
with Catherine Chambers

Raintree is an imprint of Capstone Global Library Limited, a company incorporated in England and Wales having its registered office at 7 Pilgrim Street, London, EC4V 6LB – Registered company number: 6695582

www.raintreepublishers.co.uk
myorders@raintreepublishers.co.uk

Edited by Nancy Dickmann, Adam Miller, Laura Knowles, and Helen Cox Cannons
Designed by Richard Parker and Emily Hooton at Ken Bell Graphic Design
Picture research by Mica Brancic
Production by Vicki Fitzgerald
Printed and bound in China by CTPS

ISBN 978 1 406 25978 0 (hardback)
17 16 15 14 13
10 9 8 7 6 5 4 3 2 1

ISBN 978 1 406 25983 4 (paperback)
18 17 16 15 14
10 9 8 7 6 5 4 3 2 1

British Library Cataloguing in Publication Data
Maxwell, Scott.
 Mars rover driver. -- (The coolest jobs on the planet)
 1. Roving vehicles (Astronautics)--Juvenile literature. 2. Mars (Planet)--Exploration--Juvenile literature. 3. Astronautics--Vocational guidance-- Juvenile literature.
 I. Title II. Series III. Chambers, Catherine, 1954-
 629.2'95-dc23

Acknowledgements
We would like to thank the following for permission to reproduce photographs: Alamy pp. 8 (© moodboard), 13 (© Wim Wiskerke); JPL-Caltech/Cornell/Arizona State University p. 36; NASA pp. 18 (Cornell University/Maas Digital), 5 (JPL-Caltech), 6 (JPL-Caltech/MSSS), 7, 10 (Glenn Research Center), 11, 12 (JPL-Caltech/JHU-APL), 14 (Jet Propulsion Laboratory), 15 (Glenn Research Center), 16-17 (JPL-Caltech/MSSS), 18 (Cornell University/Maas Digital), 19 (JPL-Caltech), 20, 21 (JPL-Caltech), 22 & 23 inset (Z. Gorjian, K. Kuramura, M. Stetson, E. De Jong), 26 (JPL-Caltech), 29 (JPL-Caltech/University of Arizona), 30 (JPL-Caltech), 31 (JPL/USGS), 32, 33 (JPL/University of Arizona), 34 (JPL-Caltech), 35 (JPL/Cornell/University of Arizona), 37 (JPL-Caltech), 38 (JPL-Caltech), 39 (JPL-Caltech), 41 (Lockheed Martin); Reuters p. 27 (SGVN/Sarah Reingewirtz); Scott Maxwell pp. 4, 24, 25 main & inset 25, 28, 40; Shutterstock p. 9 (© Vectomart).

Background design images supplied by Shutterstock (© Alaettin YILDIRIM, © Anelina, © Apostrophe, © Attitude, © Bill Frische, © dundanim, © Eky Studio, © Ferderic B, © Francisco Caravana, © Ghenadie, © Gl0ck, © James Steidl, © Jan Kaliciak, © justdd, © kao, © Kim Briers, © LeksusTuss, © Nataliya Hora, © oriontrail, © R-studio, © Rashevska Nataliia, © Sinelyov, © Skocko, © Sura Nualpradid, © Tjeffersion, © Uros Zunic, © Viktar Malyshchyts).

Cover pictures of an artist's concept portraying a NASA Mars Exploration Rover on the surface of Mars reproduced with permission of NASA (JPL/Cornell University).

Every effort has been made to contact copyright holders of material reproduced in this book. Any omissions will be rectified in subsequent printings if notice is given to the publisher.

Disclaimer

Millions of kilometres away, a small robot sat on a rocky planet. She'd just analysed Adirondack, a football-sized rock, and now she needed to be moved away and on to the next task. It was a crucial move. And for the first time ever, I was driving her! I managed to move her several metres – it was the most amazing and scary experience ever. The rover's name was *Spirit*, and she was my first Mars rover, so everything I did was new and exciting and heart-stopping.

I had to brush three close holes on a rock named Humphrey. So I made them into a Mickey Mouse shape using *Spirit's* RAT (Roc Abrasion Tool).

Note to self

At the end of my shift, I remember checking everything before I handed *Spirit* over to the next driver. I went home, but sleep was out of the question. I kept thinking, "Oh, wow! I've just driven a rover on Mars!" And then it hit me. Working with rovers would give me this same amazing feeling every single day!

Did you know?

Adirondack was one of the rocks we analysed. It's smooth, making it easy to grind. It's a type of basalt, a rock made through volcanic activity. We get basalt here on Earth, but on Mars it's been crumbled by water action. Adirondack is a Mohawk word meaning "tree eater", and there are certainly no trees

DREAMING AND SCHOOLING

Mars looks like a ruby in the night sky, but the red is actually wind-blown, rusty dust swirling above the planet.

When I was young, we had a tiny black-and-white TV. That little TV expanded to the size of the universe in my mind as I watched the scientific world galloping into space. I was glued to Carl Sagan's *Cosmos* series. Then there were the news reports on JPL's *Voyager* missions, which launched probes to the outer solar system from the 1970s onwards.

MY HERO!
CARL SAGAN (1934-1996)

Carl Sagan was a Professor of Astronomy and Space Sciences at Cornell University, where he took a leading role in the US Space programme. Carl briefed the *Apollo* astronauts and was closely involved in the *Voyager* missions that so inspired me. He discovered important science on Mars' climate and seasons.

From fiction to fact

I used to think of space exploration as more science fiction than science fact. *Voyager*, though, was real – people were actually doing this stuff. We couldn't send humans to different planets – they were too far away. But we were sending robots there. There was just something magical about that.

Did you know?

It was tough getting missions to Mars off the ground. The public and politicians were more interested in spending resources on the *Apollo* Moon missions and manned space travel. But in 1971, the *Mariner 9* orbiter took such great science data from Mars that the planet could be ignored no longer.

Mariner 9 took 7,329 images of Mars covering 80 per cent of its surface. It revealed dry river beds, canyons, and craters.

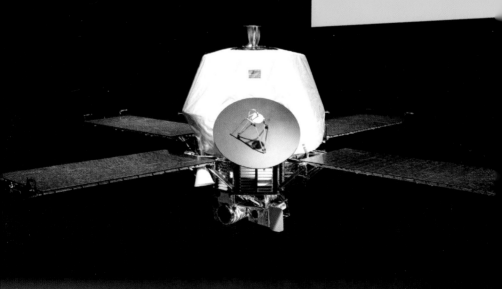

School days and star gazing

I had always been good with computers, so I went to university to study Computer Science and English. The teaching was great and the professors really cared about their students. But not many of us were aiming for NASA and the Space programme! So it was a great leap for the professors to recommend me to one of the top five US universities for studying engineering – the University of Illinois at Urbana-Champaign (UIUC), where I studied for a Master's degree in Computer Science.

Like this boy, my dad and I used to watch the night sky in the back yard. A telescope with x45 magnification will allow you to see Mars as a red disc.

TOOLS OF THE TRADE:
COMMUNICATION

Computer programming is obviously an important set of skills for handling rovers. But why study English? Because I don't just work with rovers, I work with people, too. I need to communicate with them to get across ideas and solve problems. My job also needs imagination to leap that chasm between what a rover needs to do and programming her to do it. So stick with that English class!

This is our solar system (not to scale). Earth shares it with all these other planets, which take different lengths of time to revolve around the Sun.

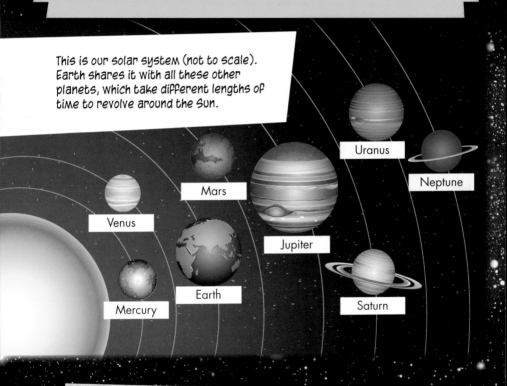

Venus

Mars

Mercury

Earth

Jupiter

Uranus

Neptune

Saturn

MY HERO!
RAY BRADBURY (1920-2012)

Ray Bradbury was one of the earliest science fiction writers. He wrote really great books like *The Martian Chronicles*. In 2009, Ray visited the Jet Propulsion Laboratory on the rovers' fifth anniversary. I asked him if he'd like to drive a rover and he agreed. Ray Bradbury never had a driving licence on Earth, but he did learn to drive on Mars!

Reaching for the stars

Writing programs means understanding computer codes and learning hundreds of algorithms. Algorithms are step-by-step instructions that allow you to carry out a task in a computer program. I had never planned to be a computer software designer for NASA, so I wasn't as well prepared as the other students at UIUC. On my first day, the professor came in with a massive book of algorithms. "Well I'm sure you all know chapters 1–6," he said, "so just prepare chapter 7 by Tuesday." I'd never seen this book in my life, and it was already Thursday! I didn't get much sleep that weekend, but I did learn all the algorithms.

This is the massive "Thumper", a computer used 60 years ago. It had far less processing power than a modern mobile phone! In the early days of space technology, computers took up so much space because large vacuum tubes or magnetic drums were needed to store data and make calculations.

This is the *Mars Observer* spacecraft. It didn't do much science on Mars, but it did take some data on energy bursts from exploding stars. Cool!

Did you know?

Mars exploration while I was a student was a bit frustrating. Scientists wanted to know more about the surface of Mars, its atmosphere and climate. So they sent up orbiters with science laboratories. The *Mars Observer* spacecraft was launched in 1992 and had great technology, but it didn't get to take much data before contact was lost.

TOOLS OF THE TRADE: COMPUTER LANGUAGES

Computer programs are written in various languages that mostly look like different flavours of simplified English. The languages have names like Python, Java, and C++. Different languages are good at different things, so it helps to know a lot of them to be able to solve different problems. It's not unusual for me to work in four or five languages in a day!

EARLY DAYS FOR ME ON MARS

My deep passion for space exploration never left me while I was at UIUC. So when a NASA JPL recruiter came from California to the University, I knew that I just had to try for it.

Geologists gather information from orbital pictures of Mars to make geological maps like these. This is the rim of the Endeavour Crater, where I've driven the rover *Opportunity*.

More ways to the top

There are so many paths into NASA. Some of our team are geologists, who study the rocks on Mars. There are chemists, too. All these scientists advise us on the targets and experiments for our rovers. On my team, we even have a sculptor! He's also a programmer, but as a sculptor he's great at imagining the rovers in 3D.

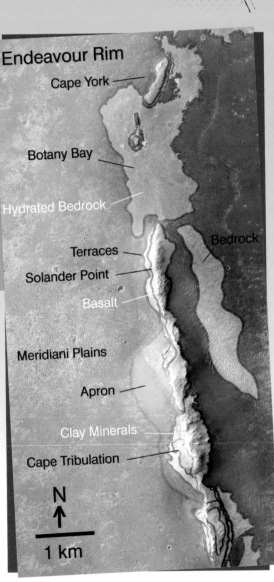

Endeavour Rim

Cape York

Botany Bay

Hydrated Bedrock

Terraces

Bedrock

Solander Point

Basalt

Meridiani Plains

Apron

Clay Minerals

Cape Tribulation

N
↑

1 km

Did you know?

Radio telescopes the size of football pitches are used to link with spacecraft. They do this by capturing radio waves that pulse from the depths of the universe. Before I worked on rovers, I learned to operate the Deep Space Network's radio telescopes. I even set up a communication pass with *Voyager 2*, now 35 years old!

This Very Large Array (VLA) radio telescope has contacted *Voyager* on its Uranus and Neptune missions via links with radio astronomy antennae as far away as Australia.

I got the job!

Wow! I was going to become a Mars rover driver! But that didn't mean learning to drive with a wheel, a joystick, or video game controls. It meant I had to learn how to program instructions for the rovers and their scientific instruments. So as well as computing, I had to use my engineering skills. Then, I had to know how to move around a copy of the rover on-screen, which is the way we drive them (see page 18 for why). But I didn't drive straight away...

This is the NASA-JPL facility at Pasadena, where I work.

Note to self

I had a lot to learn. I started as a JPL computer programmer on our multi-mission ground data system. This records and processes data for Mars missions and many others. I got the chance to be a small part of a lot of different projects. It was a total learning experience.

MY HERO!
NEIL ARMSTRONG
(1930-2012)

Neil Armstrong is my favourite
hero – among humans, that is! He
was special, not only for being
the first person on the Moon, but
also for his upstanding personal
behaviour. Armstrong began
his flight career at just 19 and
went on to become an engineer,
test pilot, astronaut, and NASA
administrator.

2003 – the Mars Exploration Rover Mission (MER)

The Mars Exploration Rover Mission (MER) was my first chance
to work on a Mars flight project. For MER's development phase,
I wrote a piece of software called the Rover Sequence Editor
(RoSE). We've used RoSE to command the rovers' spacecraft
through their seven-month cruise to Mars. Together with RoSE's
sister application, HyperDrive, we had the tools to drive rovers on
the surface.

IS THERE LIFE ON MARS?

Mars has always fascinated astronomers and scientists. Today, the planet is a harsh, frozen, nearly airless desert. It's much friendlier to robots than to humans, but it wasn't always friendly to robots, either! Good surface evidence tells us that Mars was once covered in boils of hot volcanic lava. I wouldn't want to drive a rover through that!

Mars has the tallest mountain in the solar system (Olympus Mons at 24 kilometres or 15 miles high) and the deepest canyon (Valles Marineris at 8 kilometres or 5 miles deep).

Did you know?

Two tiny moons, or satellites, orbit Mars close to its surface. Phobos orbits at 9,377 kilometres (5,826 miles) above and Deimos at 23,000 kilometres (14,292 miles). The radius of Phobos is just 11 kilometres (7 miles) and Deimos only 6 kilometres (4 miles)! These moons were discovered in 1877 by an amazing American mathematician, Asaph Hall (1829–1907).

Learning from Mars

The real question for scientists isn't "Is there life on Mars?" but "Was there life on Mars?" Mars itself could give us clues as to why it is now a desert. Could Earth become the same? This is what interests scientists.

TOOLS OF THE TRADE: PANCAMS

The views we get from the rovers' PANCAMS (panoramic cameras) are fascinating. The PANCAMS can rotate to give us a broad view of the landscape. But they can also see things human eyes can't. Used with other instruments they give our scientists information on Mars' geology (rocks and soils), topography (shape of the landscape), and meteorology (weather).

Communicating with Mars

Earth and Mars are so far apart that even when they're on the same side of the Sun it takes three minutes to get a signal from Earth to Mars. It takes another three minutes for signals to return. Sadly, this means we can't drive a rover like a remote control car! It gets a whole lot worse when Earth and Mars are at their farthest apart, on opposite sides of the Sun. Then the delay is 22 minutes each way! As my colleague Andy Mishkin says, "By the time you see the cliff coming, you've already gone over it!" That's why we program the rovers in advance – you'll find out more about this later.

The time delay between Earth and Mars means that we plan a rover's whole day at once, giving her a full science schedule.

While we sometimes wake the rover up at night for special observations, she usually sleeps through the night and spends her limited energy during the day. This photo shows a Martian sunset.

Note to self

I'm always aware that rovers ride over rocks, sands, and soft soils that look like they'd be good to drive on, but aren't! Then there are crater lips. I have to take note of all the scientists' information. Later, we'll see that the rover *Spirit* fell foul of Martian geology.

Did you know?

Martian winters are freezing cold and very dark. So I can't program a lot of tasks for the rover because her solar energy levels are low. However, I can still get her to take pictures and measurements with the robotic arm, which uses only a little power. The whole team's job here is to conserve her energy by not stressing her.

Cool tools

Now I get to tell you about the rovers' cool tools. Each rover has a robotic arm, with a shoulder, elbow, and wrist that push instruments directly up against rock and soil.

The mechanical "fist" of a rover's arm has a microscopic camera that serves the same purpose as a geologist's hand-held magnifying lens.

Did you know?

Finding iron in rocks is important. Some rocks containing iron are meteorites that have plunged to the surface of Mars from space. In other rocks, iron streaks indicate that the iron was deposited by water. This means there could have been life on Mars!

Time costs!

I'm always trying to save rover time as I work on its instructions. Even a few seconds can make a difference. Time uses up a rover's life, although we don't know how long that is. Time also costs precious mission money, which ended up at $800 million for *Spirit* and *Opportunity*. We first thought we'd only get 200 working sols (that's a Martian day) out of our rovers, so each sol was going to cost $4 million! But we've now completed over 3,000 sols on one rover and 2,210 on the other, making each sol cheaper.

Note to self

Some people think it's odd when I talk about sols. That's the word scientists use for a day on Mars, from one sunrise to the next. Why not just call it a day? Well, mainly because the Martian day is 40 minutes longer than an Earth day. It makes it too confusing to call them both "days". You need to be clear which planet you're talking about!

Cameras are mast-mounted to 1.5 metres (5 feet) high. They have a 360-degree, stereoscopic, human-like view.

Opportunity

Each tool on a rover has a scientific purpose. My job is to make sure that each move made by the rover and its tools delivers scientific evidence or results. On this photo of the rover *Opportunity*, you can find out what the tools do.

Miniature Thermal Emission Spectrometer (Mini-Tes). This identifies rocks and soils that look like they're worth examining. It can also look skyward to read Mars' atmospheric temperatures.

PANCAM reveals the landscape of Mars and uses colour filters to highlight small rocks on the surface. PANCAM can also tell us how high the dust on Mars reaches into its atmosphere.

Magnets collect magnetic dust particles for examination.

Alpha Particle X-Ray Spectrometer (APXS) looks closely at large amounts of elements present in rocks and soils.

Microscopic Imager (MI) relays high-resolution images of rocks and soils. Geologists can tell a lot about the composition of a rock from its texture and grains.

Mössbauer (MB) Spectrometer takes a close look at rocks and soils with iron in them. Mars is very rich in iron, so we can tell a lot from this instrument. The MB has its own radiation source that picks up the iron.

Rock Abrasion Tool (RAT) removes weathered rock surfaces by grinding them down. It exposes fresh soils for other instruments to examine. It's like a geologist's rock hammer and is probably the cutest tool in the kit.

A DAY IN THE LIFE

What's a normal day like for me? It is based around working while the rover rests! When it's early evening on Mars, *Opportunity* stops what she's doing. The light is fading, so her solar energy is low. She sends us images and data, and the team sets to work making those images and data into a 3D world, like a video game. This runs on our computers here on Earth. This is what we work on as we prepare *Opportunity* for her next day.

Opportunity takes microscopic images like this one. It helps geologists find out how rocks were formed.

Did you know?

Each Mars day is 24 hours and 40 minutes. This means that we can't always start work at 9.00 a.m. here on Earth as it won't often be 9.00 a.m. on

TOOLS OF THE TRADE: ROVER CHECKLIST

Our rover checklist helps us avoid problems and save time. The list now has about 50 points! We start with the state of the rover. Is she tilting? What's under her wheels? Soil? Rock? We have to find the answers to these before we move her on.

It's all about teamwork

JPL has about six engineers working on the rover at any one time, plus many more scientists and engineers on an all-day teleconference line. There are two rover drivers working together on each drive. RP1 (Rover Planner 1) develops the sequence and RP2 gives advice and consent to carry on with a move or function. In this way, everything gets checked thoroughly.

Here's the team! Teamwork is very important in this job.

Every second counts

My day involves a lot of planning and checking. This is so we can get everything right. As I said before, time costs money and rover life.

Note to self

We are in constant contact with scientists in Alabama, New York, and elsewhere, often through teleconference calls. You'd be wrong if you think our discussions are always serious. We often tease them when we've got some really great snacks to eat here at JPL – especially on doughnut Friday!

Working models of the rovers are team members, too! They help us work out if a particular manoeuvre is possible.

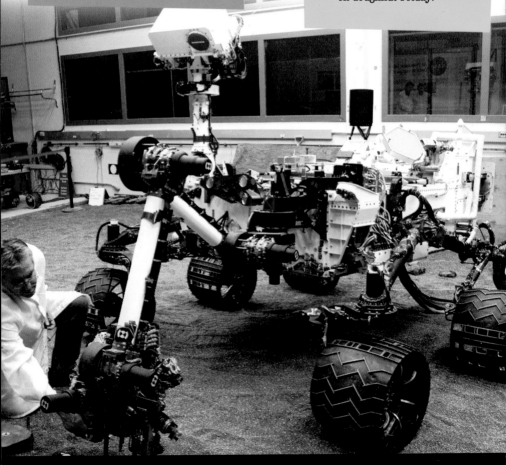

Hours 1–2 Science kick-off meeting for engineers. What's our aim for today? Do we drive? Do we use an arm to do some science research? Do we sit still and take pictures?

The kick-off team checks with the Science Operations Working Group (SOWG). What science data do they want?

We then create a software spreadsheet to plot our day. Can we do all this in the time we have? Can it be done within our rover's data volume limits?

Hours 3–4 We turn the Activity Plan into reality by roughing out a sequence of moves for the rover. Then we decide the commands needed to drive the rover, move an arm, take images, and so on.

Now it's that important time – lunch!

MY HERO!
GENTRY LEE (BORN 1942)

Gentry Lee is a brilliant engineer, and JPL's chief engineer for the Planetary Flight Systems Directorate. He gave us valuable advice when *Spirit* was stuck near the end of her life (see page 34). He's a tough critic, but you know that when you have his approval, you've done everything well!

Putting it all together

A lunch break helps avoid stress. I don't get stressed much myself, but when I do I go to the dojo (like a gym) and practise Aikido. Now back to work!

You have to learn how to "feel" the size and weight of the rover so you can drive it with the right amount of pressure.

TOOLS OF THE TRADE: SOFTWARE

The software copy of the rover on our computers is vital, as it allows us into the rover's 3D world. We have something we can control. We send commands to the software copy sitting on our desktop, and it responds like the real rover will.

Hour 4   At the Activity Plan Approval Meeting, we look at the drive animation on our rover copy to check that everything's right. It might need more detail for the sequences.

Hours 5–6   We perfect the sequence and details and then have a walkthrough meeting. The whole team looks at every command and everyone has one last chance to object (well, usually!).

Hours 7–8   I now turn the instructions into binary code (yes, the same binary code you learn about in school!) so that *Opportunity* will understand it. Then every command goes through a Sequence Report Walkthrough, which is a second chance for the team to catch any problems. Now it's ready for the rover.

Howling winds can blow soils into dunes that look like solid rock — dangerous!

Note to self

The unique thing about my job is that I always work with my software users. As a rover driver, I'm one of them myself! This helps me make better decisions about what software needs to do. It also means that when I get something wrong, I'm sure to hear about it!

EXPLORING MARS

The first missions to Mars painted a picture of a planet with sterile soils and pinky-orange skies. Scientists saw from rock and soil formations that there was the chance that water had once flowed there.

Brave *Mariners*

In the 1960s, the first Mars programme used *Mariner* spacecraft above Mars to relay images and information back to Earth. The missions were axed in the 1970s because politicians thought it too expensive. But early *Mariners* told us a lot about Mars.

In 1965, *Mariner 4's* images showed Martian craters, a thin carbon dioxide atmosphere, and a small magnetic field, which is too weak to protect the planet from the Sun's harmful emissions.

Viking warriors

The *Viking* missions of 1975 cost a lot less than the first *Mariner* series. Both *Viking I* and *Viking 2* had an orbiter, a small, cheap lander, but an expensive high-tech microbiology kit to test the soils. Basically there was more science for the dollars, which is what we're all aiming for!

Viking landers took 4,500 close images of Mars. Their orbiters took 50,000 images. Together they covered 97 per cent of Mars' surface.

TOOLS OF THE TRADE: VIKING LANDERS

Viking's landers couldn't move, but their robotic arms extended to scoop up soil. This allowed scientists to take a good look at soil and rock structure. The landers were also able to take images, make infra-red thermal maps, measure water vapour in the atmosphere, and pick up radio waves.

Did you know?

The *Viking* landers were the first to use a really important piece of computer technology. This was the ability to store the information that programmers gave them, as well as the data that they got themselves. Scientists and programmers now had more material to work on.

Getting ready to rove

NASA got some serious public support in 1977, when a young JPL team launched the two *Voyager* probes. These spacecraft sent back dazzling science from our universe. Space science was back on the map and so was landing more missions on Mars, although it took a while.

Voyagers 1 and 2 have swept past the giant planets of Jupiter, Uranus, Neptune, and 48 of their moons.

Paving the way

In 1996, the Mars *Pathfinder* mission carried a lander and its rover, *Sojourner*, to Mars. They were an experiment to see what landers and rovers could do. *Sojourner* was the first moving rover. She could only travel 10 metres (33 feet) per sol, but it really counted.

The lander relayed 16,500 images and *Sojourner* sent back 550. On top of that, she sent chemical analyses of rocks and soils, and wind and weather reports. We learned more about the planet as it once was – warm and wet with a thick atmosphere that could have sustained life.

MY HERO!
SOJOURNER TRUTH (1797-1883)

Sojourner was named after Sojourner Truth, an African-American woman who, from the 1840s, fought with great courage for civil rights. She did what seemed impossible – that's the message!

Dust devils have been spotted by orbiters such as the *Mars Global Surveyor* (MGS) and *Viking*. Some dust devils rise 8 kilometres (5 miles) into the Martian sky!

ROVERS PAST, PRESENT, AND FUTURE

We launched *Spirit* on 10 June 2003 and her mission began on 4 January 2004. It was supposed to last only until April 2004. *Spirit*, though, carried on until 2010!

Spirit's right front wheel broke about two years into her mission, but she kept on roving. In 2009, however, she rolled onto a sulphate mineral crust and fell through. *Spirit* was trapped, but she was still giving us great science! We think that the sulphate crust was transported from a volcano by flowing water. More evidence of water on Mars!

We tried 10 times to get *Spirit* out, but she was buried too deep to be saved.

Spirit's last task

We weren't able to free *Spirit* from her trap, and she didn't survive that last winter. She wasn't able to send back information on the texture of Mars' core, as we'd hoped. But on the location where she rests even now, she gently scraped away soil layer after soil layer right up until the end, for our scientists to analyse. I loved that rover and am very proud of the hard work she did for her whole life.

Spirit's journey from Sol 1 in 2004 to Sol 1506 in 2008 can be followed on this traverse map.

OSU Mapping and GIS Laboratory

Did you know?

A molten, or liquid, core is runny magnetic iron that allows electricity to pass through it. *Opportunity* has managed to pick this up through her radio signals, which help detect tiny differences in Mars' rotation. The strength of the magnetic field and the "wobbles" help us to know if the core is liquid or solid. In 2016, a lander called *InSight* will be able to do more core work.

You can see the difference between a solid core and a liquid core by spinning a hard-boiled egg on a plate and then spinning a raw egg – carefully! You'll notice that they move differently. This difference is what rovers can tune into.

The tale of *Opportunity*

In 2004, we also landed *Opportunity*. Both *Spirit* and *Opportunity* were designed to travel just 40 metres (130 feet) each day. So far, we have driven *Opportunity* further than any other rover, up to about 220 metres (722 feet) in a single day. *Opportunity* is still going strong in 2013, smashing that mission target of four months!

Here, *Opportunity* has photographed its own shadow in this dramatically lit view of the Endeavour Crater.

MY HERO!
STEVE SQUYRES
(BORN 1957)

Steve Squyres is the chief scientist for the Mars Exploration Rovers project. He is a world-leading astronomer, geologist, and nice guy.

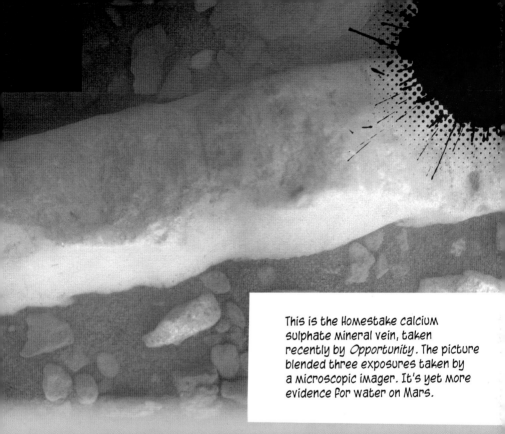

This is the Homestake calcium sulphate mineral vein, taken recently by *Opportunity*. The picture blended three exposures taken by a microscopic imager. It's yet more evidence for water on Mars.

A wounded soldier

Opportunity has had a few health problems. For a start, she's had a bad shoulder since landing, and now she can't move it directly left or right. We've also lost the use of her Mini-TES instrument, and her Mössbauer Spectrometer is now very weak. Its radiation source wears down over time, and *Opportunity* has been alive 30 times longer than expected! Her biggest problem, though, is her front right wheel. I can't drive her forward for long on it; she's only really safe going backwards. I'm very careful with *Opportunity* since *Spirit* broke her wheel.

TOOLS OF THE TRADE: WHEELS

A rover has six wheels with a motor on each. The two front and back wheels also have a steering motor. This means that when all the wheels work, the rover can turn a full circle on the spot. Rovers also have a "rocker-boogie" suspension so that if one side travels over a rock, the other side helps absorb the tilt to keep the rover stable.

A new rover!

During 2011 and 2012, I had to take a few breaks from *Opportunity* to work on the rover-driving software for the next Mars rover, called *Curiosity* . By the way, *Opportunity* is NOT being neglected. She's in the very safe hands of Julie Townsend, a really skilful rover driver who also runs an all-girl high-school robotics team.

The new kid on the block

Curiosity landed safely on Mars in August 2012 – hooray! *Curiosity* is as big as a Mini Cooper and weighs a hefty 816 kilograms (1,800 pounds). He won't roam farther or faster than our other rovers, but he'll do a better job of digging deeper below the Martian surface. *Curiosity* also carries a couple of small scientific laboratories that allow him to "taste" Mars better – like a robot tongue.

Technicians wear white bunny suits when they're building a new rover. This is so that germs from Earth don't get spread to Mars. Cute, but crucial.

Note to self

The best thing about *Curiosity* is that he has a laser on his head to burn holes in rocks! This means that you can find out from a distance what the rocks are made of, saving science time. Actually, I just think it's fun to shoot a laser on Mars!

STOP PRESS!

Curiosity touched down in Gale Crater on 5 August 2012 and underwent a "brain transplant" to change his flight software to driving and robot arm software. We're all buzzing as we busily check him out and start doing the science!

This artist's concept shows the moment that *Curiosity* touched down onto the Martian surface.

Did you know?

Spirit and *Opportunity* landed on Mars by bouncing inside air bags. We released *Curiosity* from a small spacecraft shaped like a claw that gently let the rover down. He was attached to the spacecraft by cables to make sure he didn't fall.

What next for Mars and me?

I'm so involved with *Opportunity* and *Curiosity* right now that it's hard to look ahead. But when I do, my mind explodes as I imagine rovers roaming all over the solar system! And that's what my job is really all about – reaching for those goals and working with others to turn my dreams into reality.

Note to self

I'm often asked which planet I would pick to visit in person. Well, it has to be Mars. It's a planet I know pretty well – and I have a couple of robot friends there whom I would dearly love to say hi to. I might be too old by the time we're ready for it. So through my outreach programmes I try to inspire young people – like you!

ROVER PLANNER

T1

I'm about to start driving the rover. I never quite know what each day will bring. That's why I'm smiling!

It's a big space!

Saturn and Jupiter both have moons (Titan for Saturn, Europa for Jupiter) that look like good places to explore. We might want to leave our rovers behind and send boats or submarines there, though – Titan is partly covered with poisonous methane lakes and Europa is an ice ball, with liquid slopping below the surface. Can you imagine piloting a submarine around another world's moon?

NASA is testing landing gear that will suit the conditions on Mars.

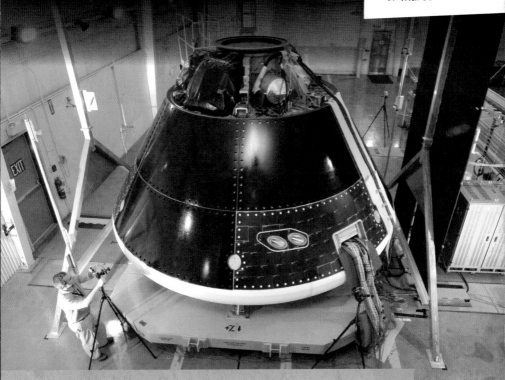

Did you know?

The future of space exploration looks awesome. We hope that the International Space Station will serve as a stepping stone for humans to travel deeper into space. Meanwhile, NASA is developing the Orion Multipurpose Crew Vehicle. That's like a bus for humans but with lots of technical equipment. One of the target destinations? Mars!

QUIZ

See how much you can remember about Mars and my work at JPL.

Questions

1. Why can't I drive a rover like I would a remote control car?

2. Why is it so important to find water on Mars and other planets?

3. Why does Mars appear red?

4. Unscramble these letters to find one of my greatest heroes:

   inarlormgntes

5. Why can't we drive rovers during Martian winters?

6. What stops sunlight from reaching the rovers' solar panels?

7. Why did *Spirit* stop working?

8. Which famous science fiction writer learned to drive a rover?

9. What is a RAT?

Answers

1. Because Mars is too far away from Earth and it would take too long for the rover to respond.

2. Because it shows that there might have been plant and animal life there.

3. Because it's surrounded by an atmosphere with rusty dust particles in it.

4. Neil Armstrong.

5. Because there is not enough sunlight to charge the rovers' solar panels. As a result, they don't have enough energy to move.

6. Windblown dust stops sunlight from reaching the rovers' solar panels.

7. *Spirit* fell through a sulphate mineral crust and we couldn't get her out.

8. Ray Bradbury was the science fiction writer who learned to drive a rover.

9. A RAT is a Rock Abrasion Tool, which removes weathered rock surfaces by grinding them down.

GLOSSARY

algorithm step-by-step instruction leading to a function to be carried out in a computer program

basalt type of volcanic rock found on Mars and on Earth

binary code computer coding system using the binary digits 0 and 1 to represent a letter, digit, or other character

calcium sulphate also known as gypsum, a volcanic mineral

canyon deep, wide split in rock, often formed by earthquakes

carbon dioxide gas in the atmosphere of Mars and Earth

core centre of a planet. It can be liquid or solid.

data facts and figures that can be used to find out more about a subject

data volume limit of information that can be held by a computer storage system

emission output of gases or other materials

geologist scientist who studies rocks and rock formations

high-resolution image with a lot of pixels in a given area. High resolution gives a sharp, focused image.

infrared rays of heat that cannot be seen by the human eye

lander vehicle that lands on a planet from a spacecraft

magnetic field space over which a magnetic force is felt. A magnetic field is measured for its strength and direction.

meteorite piece of natural material from outer space that survives its passage through Earth's atmosphere and lands on the surface

methane poisonous gas created through volcanic activity or from decaying plant matter

microbiology biology of tiny, microscopic living things. These could be as small as bacteria.

microscopic imager close-up camera with a microscope to look at the small features of rocks and soils

mineral substance solid, naturally occurring substance. Minerals are found in all living things, and in rocks and soils.

molten melted; describes the melted, oozing mineral centre of some planets' cores, or volcanoes

NASA National Aeronautics and Space Administration, responsible for the US nation's space program and for aeronautics and aerospace research

orbiter spacecraft that revolves around a planet high above its surface

PANCAM high-resolution, stereo camera that rotates to give broad colour pictures

probe scientific space explorer that leaves Earth to discover more about the solar system

radiation waves of invisible energy that move through a space or material

radiation source origin of energy waves, for example the Sun, space, or a planet's core

radio telescope large disc that captures radio waves from the depths of the universe

robotic arm arm attached to a robot that can be programmed to move and perform functions

sequence set of moves or instructions planned in a certain order to achieve a particular aim

sol full day and night on Mars that lasts for 24 hours and 40 minutes

solar energy light and heat that radiates from the Sun. We use it as an energy source through solar panels.

solar system the Sun and all the planets, moons, and other bodies that orbit around it

spreadsheet computer page with grids and columns used to create tables and plans

stereoscopic camera with more than one lens. It creates images that are three-dimensional (3D).

sterile without life

sulphate yellow mineral that is not a metal. It often comes out of volcanoes.

walkthrough examine each stage of a process in detail, to make sure that the process will work when it is actually carried out

weathered worn down by the action of wind, water, heat, or ice

FIND OUT MORE

Books

Astronomy (100 Facts), Sue Becklake (Miles Kelly, 2011)
Space: A Children's Encyclopedia (Dorling Kindersley, 2010)
Space, Black Holes and Stuff, Glenn Murphy (Macmillan, 2010)

Websites

mars.jpl.nasa.gov/explore/spirit
Learn more about the rover *Spirit*.

www.nasa.gov/mission_pages/msl/index.html
Catch up with *Curiosity's* life on Mars as it happens now.

www.nhm.ac.uk/nature-online/virtual-wonders/vrmars.html
Watch a virtual Mars globe spin and take a look at its mountains and craters. The globe shows an accurate map of Mars taken by the *Mars Global Surveyor* and the MOLA Mars missions. Use the links to find out more about the universe.

solarsystem.nasa.gov/kids/index.cfm
Click on this website and take a trip around the solar system!

voyager.jpl.nasa.gov
This is a really cool website about *Voyagers 1* and *2*. On the right-hand side of the web page, you can track the *Voyagers'* distance from Earth and the Sun.

DVD

The Wonders Collection, Brian Cox (BBC, 2011)
This is a box set of awesome space science and images.

Places to visit

Royal Observatory Greenwich
Blackheath Avenue
London SE10 8XJ
www.rmg.co.uk/royal-observatory
Visit the cool planetarium at the Royal Observatory at Greenwich in London.

World Museum
William Brown Street
Liverpool L3 8EN
www.liverpoolmuseums.org.uk/wml/collections/physical-sciences/space.aspx
Visit the Liverpool Museum to see their Space section.

Science Museum
South Kensington, London, SW7 2DD
www.sciencemuseum.org.uk/visitmuseum/galleries/space.aspx
Explore our galaxy and get close up to replica rockets, satellites, space probes, and landers.

National Space Centre
Exploration Drive, Leicester LE4 5NS
www.spacecentre.co.uk
This has so much – a planetarium plus galleries of rockets, space suits, meteorites, and even videoconference sessions with astronauts such as Timothy Peake.

Glasgow Science Centre
50 Pacific Way, Glasgow GS1 1EA
www.gsc.org.uk
This has a great planetarium and you can learn a lot in the stargazer sessions.

Armagh Planetarium
College Hill, Armagh, County Armagh BT61 9DB
www.armaghplanet.com
This planetarium has some great video shows of the universe.

INDEX